PERSONAL COUNSELING: A FIFTY-MINUTE GUIDE

Elwood N. Chapman

and

Richard L. Knowdell

CRISP PUBLICATIONS, INC.
Los Altos, California

YOUR ATTITUDE IS SHOWING

We are not always conscious that we *show* our mental attitudes to others. So that we may become more aware of this, the drawings in this book have been designed to resemble the tiny amoeba.

To refresh your memory, the microscopic amoeba is constantly changing size and shape, and is often referred to as a beginning form of life. Each amoeba you see is reflecting an attitude.

Their purpose in this publication is to remind you of how important a positive attitude is in counseling.

E.N. Chapman

"After all, I'm just an amoeba."

CREDITS
Editor: **Michael Crisp**
Designer: **Carol Harris**
Typesetting: **Interface Studio**
Cover Design: **Carol Harris**

Copyright © 1986 by Crisp Publications, Inc.
Printed in the United States of America

Library of Congress Catalog Card Number 86-70065
Chapman, Elwood N. and Knowdell, Richard L.
Personal Counseling: A Fifty-Minute Guide
ISBN O-931961-14-9

PREFACE

Most books on counseling are written for professionals, psychologists, clinicians, or others seeking certification as professional counselors. Yet, almost everyone becomes involved in counseling in a more informal sense. Thus most people need to understand and be able to apply basic (non-clinical) techniques of good counseling.

PERSONAL COUNSELING is designed for the lay person. Although it teaches some of the techniques and principles used by professionals, it was written for managers, supervisors, financial and retirement counselors, law officers, or parents—**Anyone who needs to learn good counseling techniques even though they do not have the time to take courses prepared for professionals. It is also ideal for peer counseling.**

This book is designed to be read with a pencil. You will be encouraged to complete a number of exercises that provide an opportunity to apply the concepts presented. Once completed, you can strengthen your counseling skills even further by using the material presented for review and follow-up.

GOOD LUCK!

VOLUNTARY
CONTRACT*

I, _____ , hereby agree to
(Your name)

meet with the individual designated below within thirty days

to discuss my progress toward incorporating the counseling

techniques and ideas presented in this program. The purpose

of this meeting will be to *review* areas of strength and

establish action steps for areas where improvement may

still be required.

_____

Signature

I agree to meet with the above individual on

_____

Month   *Date*   *Time*

at the following location.

_____

_____

Signature

*The purpose of this agreement is to motivate you to
incorporate important concepts and techniques into your daily
activities. It also provides a degree of accountability between
you and the person you select to sign the agreement.

CONTENTS

COUNSELING IS A PROVEN WAY TO HELP
OTHERS SORT OUT AND SOLVE PROBLEMS.
COUNSELING IS USUALLY ACCOMPLISHED
PRIVATELY ON A ONE-ON-ONE BASIS. THERE
IS NO MAGIC TO THE TECHNIQUES, METHODS,
AND PRINCIPLES OF COUNSELING. THEY CAN
BE LEARNED AND APPLIED BY ANYONE.

MEET SOME SUCCESSFUL COUNSELORS

MEET SOME FAILURES

MAKE YOUR CHOICE NOW

SUCCESSES	FAILURES

THOSE WHO:

Learn
Those who learn, then use accepted counseling techniques

Those who act without learning basic counseling techniques

Accept
Those who acknowledge the worth of the person counseled regardless of the situation

Those who reject a person counseled because of the situation, i.e. "How stupid!"

Listen
One who listens to hear **all** the person being counseled has to say

One who listens only superficially, and quickly jumps to conclusions

Confirm
Those who paraphrase or repeat back what they **think** the other person said

Those who inject their own interpretation of what the person meant to say

Are Optimistic
Individuals who look for reasons and techniques to make things work

Those who decide things won't and can't work

Are Objective and Non-judgmental
Those who assess the usefulness of what a person has done without assigning blame

Those who see activities as either right or wrong; good or bad

Are Confidential
One who has the ability to not reveal what has been said during "counseling"

Those who gossip or reveal to others, what has been said during private "counseling"

Promote Decision-Making
One who can provide tools that will assist a person to make his or her own decision

Those who make decisions for the person being counseled

Support
Those who offer a person support after the decision is made

Those who say "I told you so" when a decision doesn't work out

————————————————

————————————————

————————————————

————————————————

OPPORTUNITIES

HUMAN CONFLICTS

Everyone has had conflicts involving other people. There is no escape. Although not all human conflicts can be resolved, counseling usually offers the best hope. Someone, however, must **initiate** the private discussion. If you are a supervisor and one of your employees has become a problem, you are the one who should intervene and see if the problem can be solved through counseling. If you have a problem with a friend over whom you have no authority, you can **still** initiate a communication session (counseling) that may help resolve things. Once you learn basic counseling skills–and learn how to use them–you will develop more confidence. All of this should help reduce the amount of human conflict in <u>your</u> life.

WHERE COUNSELING SKILLS CAN BE PUT TO USE

Most of us are surrounded with opportunities to become counselors. Learning to recognize and become involved in those we encounter can enhance our careers and personal lives. Place a check in those areas that provide you with opportunities for ''counseling.''

☐ **FORMAL SUPERVISOR:** A foreman or manager in a position to assist an employee to solve a work-related or personal problem. (Counseling is recognized as a vital management tool and most supervisors use counseling almost daily. People ''in charge'' of others often find it necessary to invite people into counseling sessions).

☐ **INFORMAL SUPERVISOR:** A scout leader or athletic coach whose expertise generates credibility even about unrelated problems. (Anyone responsible for the behavior of others need some basic counseling skills).

☐ **ADVISOR IN A BUSINESS SITUATION:** A banker, insurance agent, or financial counselor who is often the first ''outsider'' to learn a customer is facing a problem. (The customer may be seeking advice or assistance where you are in a position to help. With the proper skills, you can provide the required counseling. Without them, you can refer the customer to a professional counselor who can help).

☐ **FRIEND OR NEIGHBOR:** A friend who observes when a person is troubled by something. This is the most sensitive of all areas because the individual may not have sought your counsel. A non-directive approach is usually best; keeping your feelings in the background. (Good listening skills are essential).

☐ **PARENT OR RELATIVE:** An individual who is approached by a family member in search of an objective opinion. (If you decide to help a family member, you will need the skills provided in *Personal Counseling*. Counseling a relative also calls for a non-directive approach that maximizes listening skills).

Case studies help provide insights you may not already possess. Five case problems are included in this program. Please give each your careful attention.

The case on the opposite page will help you understand some items involved in becoming a successful counselor.

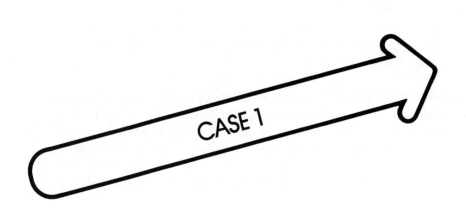

CASE 1

WHO WILL MAKE THE BEST COUNSELOR?

Byron and Ginger are new supervisors for a large service organization. On Friday both will attend a company-sponsored seminar designed to teach effective counseling skills to deal with problem employees and enhance productivity. Byron views the day as an opportunity to contribute; Ginger has some misgivings.

Byron has already demonstrated good management skills. He is excellent at delegating, setting priorities, making decisions and communicating—especially in group situations. Byron is a high-tempo supervisor who knows how to build strong relationships with superiors. It is also obvious that Byron cares for people, especially his own employees. In his younger days, he spent several summers as a camp counselor. Although a Business Administration major at the University, his early interest in people caused him to minor in psychology.

Ginger is as qualified as Byron academically (she was an accounting major with a minor in data processing) however her future appears more limited. Where Byron likes to be out front, Ginger prefers to stay in the background and let her accomplishments speak for themselves. Ginger is not as good at group communication, and is content to participate in less-obvious ways. She is not looking forward to Friday because she feels the word counselor implies someone who uses psychological techniques to manipulate others. Ginger is an outstanding listener who is extremely patient with her employees; however, she does not view herself as a counselor. She wants to build a strong, efficient staff, but feels uncomfortable giving advice, especially when it is of a personal nature. During her first formal appraisal Ginger's superior wrote on the rating form: ''Outstanding learner.''

Grade Byron and Ginger on how skillful they will be at using basic counseling skills (review Page 5). Assign a letter grade of A, B, C, D, or F.

SKILL	BYRON	GINGER
Learning	_____	_____
Accepting	_____	_____
Listening	_____	_____
Confirming/Repeating	_____	_____
Displaying Optimism	_____	_____
Being Objective/Non-Judgmental	_____	_____
Staying Confidential	_____	_____
Promoting Decision-Making	_____	_____
Offering Support	_____	_____

Who do you think will become the better counselor? Turn to page 57 for the view of the authors.

COUNSELING IS A COMMUNICATIONS CHALLENGE!

Unfortunately the term counselor is often misinterpreted. Some think only of authority figures such as lawyers and psychiatrists. Others believe a person can only become a counselor after formal training.

In reality a counselor is an advisor and interviewer, who communicates on a one-on-one basis. A counselor can talk seriously with another person about a problem or situation.

Chances are good you are **already** involved in counseling. In approximately fifty minutes, you should be better prepared to counsel others.

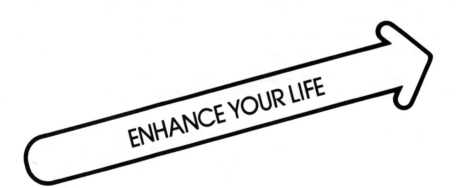

ENHANCE YOUR LIFE

WHAT CAN BECOMING A GOOD COUNSELOR OR ADVISOR DO FOR YOU?

People underestimate the advantages in learning how to become a skillful one-to-one communicator. More than you may think, developing this skill could be your *key* to a better future. Place a check in the square opposite those statements that are important to you.

☐   1.   Becoming a better counselor can help improve my career opportunities.

☐   2.   Learning to counsel others will add to my personal confidence.

☐   3.   Learning to work with others on a one-on-one basis will improve my communication skills.

☐   4.   Helping others will give me more personal satisfaction and self-respect

☐   5.   Becoming a better advisor will help me build better, more rewarding relationships.

☐   6.   Improving counseling skills will help me become a better parent, and/or leader.

☐   7.   Learning to counsel will help me recognize and solve my own problems.

☐   8.   Helping others will make me feel I am making a contribution.

☐   9.   Working as a counselor will help me improve critical listening skills.

☐   10.   Counseling others will help me better understand myself.

''I have found that the best way to give advice to your children is to find out what they want and then advise them to do it.''
Harry S. Truman

YOU DO NOT NEED TO BE AN EXTROVERT TO BE A SUCCESSFUL COUNSELOR. QUIET, THOUGHTFUL PEOPLE OFTEN ARE MORE SUCCESSFUL.

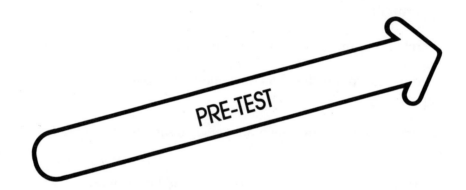

RATING PERSONAL "COUNSELING" SKILLS

This exercise is designed to measure your basic counseling skills. At this stage don't worry if you have a less than perfect score. After you have had an opportunity to practice the counseling skills covered in this book you will be able to measure your progress by taking this exercise again.

Read each statement, and then circle the number you feel best fits you.

		Disagree			Agree	
1.	I need to practice a newly learned skill before I use it "for real."	1	2	3	4	5
2.	I can accept others as worthy individuals even if I don't like aspects of their behavior.	1	2	3	4	5
3.	I can wait until I hear all a person has to say before I form an opinion and decide on a response.	1	2	3	4	5
4.	When appropriate, I will paraphrase what a person has said to confirm that I heard them accurately.	1	2	3	4	5
5.	I am generally optimistic, and look for possible solutions rather than roadblocks.	1	2	3	4	5
6.	I try to understand behavior objectively before branding it as "good" or "bad".	1	2	3	4	5
7.	People who know me trust me to keep a confidence.	1	2	3	4	5
8.	I try to help friends make their own decisions, rather than ask them to accept what I think is the best solution.	1	2	3	4	5
9.	I am someone people feel they can turn to in troubled times for support.	1	2	3	4	5

SCORING: If you scored under thirty, you will most likely benefit from learning and applying the counseling skills presented in this book.

There is no evidence that it takes a prescribed mix of personality traits to be a successful counselor.

YOU HAVE THE RIGHT STUFF

PERSONAL TRAITS OF SUCCESSFUL COUNSELORS

Below are ten personality traits found in successful counselors. Place a plus in the square opposite those you already possess; a check mark opposite those you feel can be better developed in the future; and a question mark in any remaining squares.

☐ Patient

☐ Perceptive and sensitive

☐ Like people

☐ Non-threatening demeanor

☐ Sense of humor

☐ Desire to help

☐ Positive attitude

☐ Good listener

☐ Warm personality

☐ Problem Solver

THINK OF COUNSELING AS A HIGHLY-DEVELOPED SKILL SUCH AS REPAIRING A FINE WATCH. INSTEAD OF SELECTING MECHANICAL TOOLS, YOU SELECT THE RIGHT WORDS AND DELIVER THEM AT THE RIGHT TIME IN THE RIGHT WAY.

COUNSELING SKILLS

COUNSELING SKILLS

We have read about some personal traits of successful counselors. Now let us look at some skills of successful counselors.

Below are nine counseling skills. To the right of the characteristic, indicate how you feel you would be rated.

Characteristic	I possess this characteristic	I am developing this characteristic	I am not sure that I can develop this characteristic
1. Will learn from Experience			
2. Able to Accept Others			
3. Good Listening Skills			
4. Will Test Assumptions			
5. Have Optimistic Outlook			
6. Can Be Non-Judgmental			
7. Can Keep A Confidence			
8. Will Encourage Decisions			
9. Can Be Supportive			

TRUE COUNSELING TAKES PLACE WHEN BOTH PARTIES DEVOTE THEMSELVES TO SOLVING A PROBLEM. COUNSELING IS MORE THAN A FEW MOMENTS OF A CASUAL CONVERSATION.

THE 5 R's OF COUNSELING

DOING IT RIGHT

WHY?	**THE RIGHT PURPOSE.** Counseling is a way to solve problems that have not or will not solve themselves in other ways. Sometimes the counselor (supervisor, parent, advisor, friend) will initiate the process—sometimes the individual will seek assistance voluntarily. Whenever talking things over will help—**the purpose is right**.
WHEN?	**THE RIGHT TIME.** Counseling is often a sensitive process. Arranging the best time for both parties will set the stage for successful discussion. The right time seldom happens by accident. (It is not a good time for a parent to counsel a teenager about missing curfew at two a.m).
WHERE?	**THE RIGHT PLACE.** Whether in a living room, office, or on a park bench, the location should be relaxing, quiet, private, and free from interruptions (including telephone). It would be difficult to have a productive, confidential counseling session on the subway.
WHAT?	**THE RIGHT APPROACH.** The serious nature of counseling can cause both parties to be "uneasy" at the beginning. Developing a non-threatening reassuring approach is important. People talk more freely when they do not feel threatened.
HOW?	**THE RIGHT TECHNIQUES.** Every counseling situation is different. An advisor must be sensitive to what is involved and proceed accordingly. Sometimes a direct "lets get down to business" approach is called for—sometimes a non-directive "its great to see you again" approach is best. The idea is to use the best techniques throughout the process. This program will help provide the techniques for you to do this.

COUNSELING STYLE

When you assume the role of a counselor, picture yourself in a private comfortable room discussing a problem with a friend. Be comfortable and relaxed.

It is vital for you to feel good about your personality and style. Be yourself. If you try to be somebody else (a lawyer or psychologist), it will probably be awkward, and you will communicate poorly.

TIPS AHEAD

THE PSYCHOLOGY OF COUNSELING

Here are some tips to help you learn ways to become a good counselor.

Be A Guide, Not The Leader—Your role is to guide others to decisions that will be best for *them*. You don't make the decision, they do. Although two heads are often better than one, your head should play a minor role.

Be Someone Who Helps Another Resolve A Problem—A problem burdens the other party, not you. When you help a person solve that problem, you lighten the burden they carry. It is a win-win situation. They feel better, and you feel rewarded about the role you played in the process.

Promote Self-Esteem—You may need to instill some self-confidence and build self-esteem in the other party before they can sort out and solve their problems. When you listen respectfully and say the right things at the right time, you make others more capable. Sometimes this is the key for a good solution.

Be A Person Who Takes The Initiative—Intervention counseling is difficult. When another party seeks you out for advice, everything is in your favor. The "climate" is usually positive. However, when you must intervene because a person's problem is causing distress (or lower productivity) among others, you have a more difficult challenge. When you are successful with intervention counseling everyone comes out ahead.

Foster Independence, Not Dependence—Counseling assumes a different dimension when you attempt to help a party you supervise or live with. In such cases it is a good idea to keep the **Mutual Reward Theory** in mind. The idea is to make sure you and the other party receive rewards from each other and that the reward system is understood. Identifying such rewards during a counseling session can be productive. Once identified—and the rewards are earned—a relationship is strengthened and further counseling may not be necessary.

COUNSELING CAN BE COMPARED
TO PLAYING BASEBALL

- Every session presents a new ball game.

- You can't win them all.

- Sometimes it takes more than one time at bat to be successful.

- Four basic essentials (bases) need to be covered in each meeting to achieve maximum results.

COUNSELING STRATEGIES AHEAD

COVER ALL THE BASES IN SUCCESSFUL COUNSELING

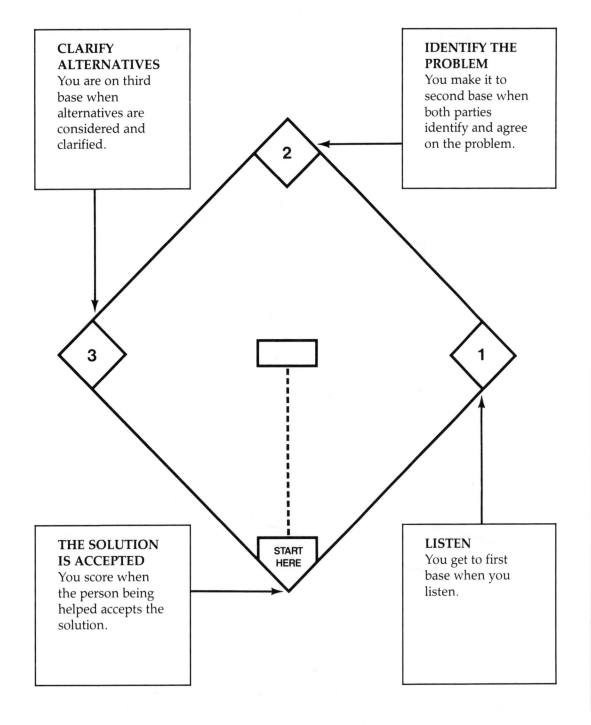

CLARIFY ALTERNATIVES
You are on third base when alternatives are considered and clarified.

IDENTIFY THE PROBLEM
You make it to second base when both parties identify and agree on the problem.

THE SOLUTION IS ACCEPTED
You score when the person being helped accepts the solution.

LISTEN
You get to first base when you listen.

START HERE

TIP ON HOW TO
GET TO FIRST BASE:
MAKE YOUR APPROACH
QUIET, FRIENDLY, PERCEPTIVE,
AND POSITIVE.

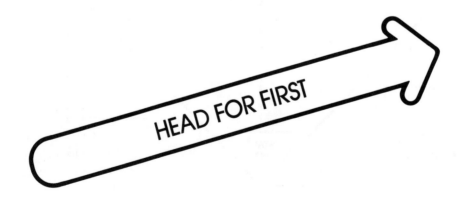

HEAD FOR FIRST

FIRST BASE: THE SKILL OF LISTENING

Achieving rapport with the other party will get you to first base. Following are nine tips to help you get there.

The NINE Steps To First Base

1. Send friendly non-verbal signals

2. Give a warm and sincere greeting

3. Demonstrate an immediate desire to help

4. Listen to what is being said

5. Listen to what is <u>not</u> being said

6. Listen to what ''can't'' be said

7. Don't make a judgement too quickly

8. Listen with your ears, eyes <u>and</u> your body

9. Ask quality questions to better learn the situation

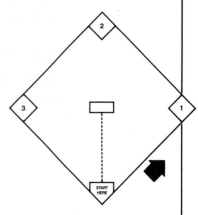

**THE LESS TALKING YOU DO AS A COUNSELOR
THE MORE EFFECTIVE YOU WILL BE**

INTERVENTION COUNSELING

Waiting for time to solve a problem is a luxury one can not always afford. This is especially true in the workplace where productivity standards must be achieved. It is equally true in personal situations where the behavior of one individual is destructive to another. Under such circumstances, a meeting needs to be initiated.This is called intervention counseling and often puts counseling skills to a demanding test.

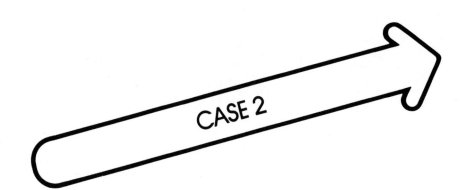

CASE 2

WHICH APPROACH IS BEST?

Justine is increasingly upset over Sally's on-the-job behavior. Employed six weeks ago (at Justine's suggestion) Sally is not living up to her potential. The primary problem seems to be Sally's inability to separate her responsibilities at work with her personal problems. She has been late and absent more than any other member of the staff, and she receives far too many phone calls from her children. What makes the situation even more irritating to Justine is the fact that this problem was anticipated and discussed during the employment interview. Sally said: "You need not worry about my home problems. Things are under control."

Justine has asked Sally to join her in her office in ten minutes. She is reviewing the 5 R's of counseling to decide which of the following approaches to take.

Approach #1: Use a directive technique. During the first few minutes reflect on the conversation that took place during the interview and then list items that have been taking place. Once this has been done, then ask the question: "What are you going to do about it?"

Approach #2: Use a non-directive technique. Sit back, say very little, and ask Sally how things are going. Do not mention the home situation unless it comes from her. Do not mention that being late and absent is causing problems unless Sally wants to talk about it. Sally will probably feel uncomfortable and do 90% of the talking.

Approach #3: Employ the "I'm disappointed" strategy. Say in a non-threatening way that things are not working out and you thought it best to discuss it. The idea behind this approach is to discover how intense the "home problem" may be so a solution might be fashioned.

Select the approach that you feel will best lead to a solution to the problem.

I vote for Approach #1 ☐   Approach #2 ☐   Approach #3 ☐

See page 57 for views of the Authors.

TO REACH SECOND BASE IT IS NECESSARY TO DISCOVER THE PROBLEM

Skillful counselors learn how to look beneath and beyond what people say. They seek hidden causes or misunderstandings that the person being counseled may be unable to sense because they are too close to the problem. Counselors learn to uncover these important aspects by asking the right questions, at the right time, and in the right manner.

EASY AS YOU GO!

IDENTIFY THE PROBLEM:

A problem needs to be seen clearly and understood before it can be solved. Your role as a counselor is to help others do this. The following suggestions should help.

Talking is therapeutic. People who want help usually have a deep need to talk things out. The more they do this in your presence the better. Be sure to provide them with sufficient time to get things out of their system.

The blame game. Sometimes individuals need to blame others for predicaments before they understand that they, themselves may be responsible. Give those you counsel time to do this. Do not become irritable during the process. It is often a hurdle that must be overcome before a person is ready to assume a different kind of behavior.

Problems are seen more clearly through verbalization. It is one thing to think things out in your head; it is something different to talk things out in front of another. Talking sometimes provides insights not possible through self-analysis. Keep reminding yourself that as a person talks she or he may be coming closer to an understanding of the problem.

Most problems involve relationships with others. Human conflicts are the most difficult to satisfactorily resolve. While listening to such a problem, it is important not to take sides. Although the individual you are working with may be partially at fault (there are usually two sides to any human conflict), it will take time for the person to sense it. Realization of the problem will often be recognized when alternatives to solve the conflict are studied.

**Things to Keep in Mind
When Going Toward Second Base**

1. Listen and be patient

2. Accept and don't judge

3. Question or restate for clarification

4. Remain objective

COUNSELING OBJECTIVITY

It is said that the closer someone is to you, the more difficult it becomes to advise that person. It is often more problematical for a mother to counsel her daughter than it would be to counsel someone else's daughter. The reason for this is because your emotions get tangled up in the counseling process. Generally speaking, the more objective the counselor, the better the results.

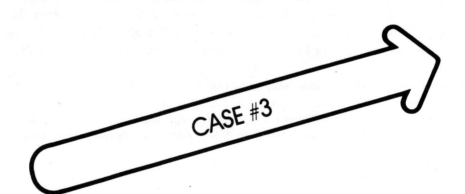

CASE #3

WILL GRAY GET TO SECOND BASE WITH HIS SON?

When it comes to his son, Tony, Gray has two primary goals. First, he wants to maintain a good father-son relationship. Second, he wants Tony to mature into a responsible adult. The situation is complicated because Gray and Tony's mother divorced two years ago, and Tony lives with his mother.

Last night his ex-wife called and asked Gray to counsel their son on a series of problems including hostility toward school and his insistence that he is old enough to have his own car. Tony turned sixteen two months ago.

Gray has arranged to spend Saturday afternoon with Tony. His plan is to take his son to a professional soccer game (Tony plays soccer in high school) and then sit in a quiet restaurant later to talk things over. His approach (once both are comfortable) is to say, "Tony, your mother says things are not going too well for you right now. I thought we might talk about it."

Once Tony starts talking, Gray hopes to accomplish the following.

1. Discover problems as Tony sees them.

2. Try to sense how the problems are interrelated.

3. Discover what Tony feels would solve the problems.

4. Find out *why* Tony thinks the solution (or solutions) would work.

If this is satisfactorily accomplished, Gray intends to delay his support of one solution over another until the following week. This will give him time to evaluate the options. It will also give him an opportunity to talk with his ex-wife. He feels strongly that both should be involved in whatever solution may be reached.

How does Gray plan to get to second base? Will his strategy get them there?_____

_____

Compare your answer to that of the authors on page 57.

MAKE THE MOVE
TO THIRD BASE

CHALLENGE AHEAD!

THE ELEGANT SOLUTION

To most problems there are what professionals call elegant solutions. This is the **"ideal** solution" under the circumstances. It usually means that the person involved can live with the decision and others will not be hurt beyond reason. Your job as a counselor is to help another to isolate the problem, fashion a solution and accept it as their own. This is a sensitive process that requires you to understand the feelings of the other party. It is not always easy for a person to accept a solution–even though it may be the best one under the circumstances.

COUNSELING IS THE ABILITY TO HELP OTHERS THROUGH THE DECISION-MAKING PROCESS

ONE STEP THAT MUST BE TAKEN IS TO CLAIFY THE ALTERNATIVES

Your role as an advisor is to help others *weigh and decide* which road to take. Academic counselors assist students in the selection of the right courses. Marriage counselors help individuals decide how to satisfactorily resolve marital problems. Supervisors help keep employees productive and positive.

Whatever your role, the counselor should emphasize the *weighing* part of the process, and let the other party do the *deciding*. Here are some suggestions.

Get several alternatives on the table. Frequently an advisor can suggest an alternative not previously considered by the person being counseled. In most situations possibilities are greater than first perceived.

The weighing process is complex. To *weigh* means to compare and balance one possibility against all others. In a counseling situation this means plenty of discussion. Often the advisor must lead the party into the process, and then record reactions of one alternative to another. Some minds are more capable of weighing than others. As a counselor, you need to concentrate on this part of the process.

Discarding alternatives. As a counselor, try to keep the party from throwing out possibilities prematurely. On the other hand when a solution is obviously not close to being ''elegant,'' it should be discarded quickly. If you get alternatives down to the ''rule of three'' the efficiency of the process will improve. Weighing three possibilities is much easier than five or six.

Making the decision. If you listen and observe, you will get signals that suggest which solution is best for the party being counseled. These signals—plus your own understanding of the problem can help direct the person counseled to the ideal solution. Still—the decision must be made by the other party, not you. Do not rush the process. In many cases you will find yourself protecting the other party by asking him or her to carefully ''think it over''.

VOICE CONTROL

Effective counselors, like actors and actresses, quickly learn to appreciate the importance of their voices. An agitated, loud voice is upsetting to the person being helped. A quiet, modulated voice contributes measurably to the right counseling atmosphere. It is an excellent idea for anyone preparing to improve his or her counseling techniques to tape record and listen carefully to the tone of that voice. Even better, "mock" counseling sessions with a friend (going around the four bases of a problem) followed by a critique can improve self-confidence and a better "counseling style." This kind of practice is highly recommended.

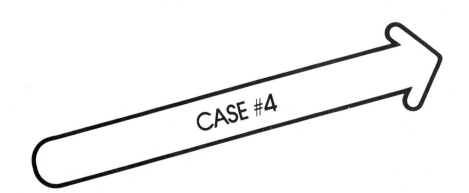

CASE #4

LETTING THE CLIENT MAKE THE CHOICE

Clergyman Stacy received a call from John and Mary Jones yesterday requesting a counseling appointment. One was arranged for this afternoon. Both John and Mary have been active church members for over twenty years. They have never asked for counseling before.

The approach was easy but the anxiety on Mary's face was obvious. John seemed depressed. Getting them to talk openly about the problem took time but it eventually came out. John has had a deepening conflict with his superior at work and has been threatened with dismissal. His boss was recently promoted to president of the company, and now has even more control over John's future. Clergyman Stacy knew how serious the conflict was when John admitted he had been on sedatives for several months. After an hour of discussion, Clergyman Stacy made the move to third base by saying: "Let's list the alternatives to this unfortunate situation."

Through discussion, the following possibilities were listed:

- Try to hang in for three years in order to take an early retirement
- Seek a transfer within the corporation, so he would not have to report to the president
- Accept a lower position with less pressure
- Retire now
- Resign and make a career change
- Initiate an age-discrimination suit (John is 59)

A confrontation with John's superior was ruled out because John tried this on one occasion and all that happened was a more intense, hate-filled relationship. The conflict seems to be irreconcilable.

After a discussion of each alternative, it was decided to narrow choices to the three year "sweat out" period, seek a transfer, or retire now. John cannot bring himself to a lower position, and he is not up to a career change. An age discrimination suit would add more stress and push John into deeper psychological turmoil. Noticing, at this point, that both John and Mary seem pleased with the progress but fatigued beyond the point of being able to make a sound decision, Clergyman Stacy suggests that all three study and evaluate the remaining alternatives and meet again the following afternoon.

How would you rate Clergyman Stacy as a counselor?

Excellent ☐   Good ☐   Weak ☐

Compare your rating with that of the author on page 57.

END OF COUNSELING SESSION GOALS

You will know you are approaching home base when the following occurs:

The person you are helping can see the light (solution) at the end of the tunnel.

The individual has developed the necessary confidence to select the best available alternative and make a decision.

The person's burden has been (at least partially) lifted. Self-esteem has been restored.

GETTING HOME SAFELY

CLOSING THE SESSION

It is usually up to the counselor to terminate the counseling. This process starts on third base where (hopefully) alternatives have been isolated. As you help the person you are counseling select the elegant solution, consider weaving the following steps into your style:

Ask the individual to restate and review the decision. This is important because it insures that an agreement has been reached. If necessary, the counselor may wish to articulate the implications of the decision. **(Skill: ask/listen/accept).**

Help to reinforce the individual's self-esteem. Whether a decision has been reached or not (sometimes it takes additional sessions), it is important that the party leaves feeling better. Counseling should be an uplifting experience for both parties. Always compliment the person being counseled toward the end of the session. State you are encouraged with the progress. **(Skill: be optimistic/supportive).**

Discuss how solution is to be implemented. In most situations, the counselor can make suggestions about how the person can proceed in the future. These are often little things that can be said easily. The session has produced the right road to take, now it is permissible to provide certain warnings about possible detours, sharp turns, etc. **(Skill: promote confidence in decisions).**

Leave door open for return visit. Counselors more often than not build lasting relationships with those they assist. This makes it easy for the individual to return voluntarily. Even so, an invitation to return is reinforcing. An experienced counselor knows that a single counseling session seldom solves a major problem. A return visit to you, the counselor, is a compliment. **(Skill: accept/support).**

ADVANCE PLANNING

In certain situations a counselor knows in advance that a difficult session is inevitable. Trouble is on the horizon. Under these conditions it is possible, and sometimes advisable, for the counselor to devise a "game plan" in advance. The danger in doing this is a loss of flexibility. The counselor might try so hard to make the game plan work that he or she does not listen to the other party, and the actual problem never gets identified or resolved. It may be advisable to go into a session with a plan; but once communication starts, it is usually better to play things by ear. Counselors with preconceived ideas are often their own worst enemies.

CASE #5

COUNSELING STRATEGY

No question about it. Wayne is the best quarterback Valley High has had in a decade, but the publicity has apparently inflated his ego. As a result, Wayne is no longer a good team player. He is frequently late to practice, and resentment against Wayne among team players is growing.

With league playoffs just two weeks away (Valley High has already qualified), Coach Jennings is disturbed. Without Wayne their chances are poor. However unless Wayne changes his attitude, the rest of the team may not perform up to potential. After thinking it over, the coach decides on this strategy.

Tomorrow, after practice, he will ask Wayne to come by his office. Using a non-directive approach, Coach Jennings hopes to get an open conversation started where he can point out to Wayne that college scouts will be present during the playoffs, and that Wayne needs the support of the entire team to look his best. He plans to cover all the bases with Wayne, hoping he will get the picture without having to spell things out.

If Wayne doesn't get rid of his cocky attitude as a result of this session, Coach Jennings will use a directive approach. He will get tough and lay it on the line with Wayne. He will communicate that he will not stand for Wayne's behavior and will demand a positive change or ''bench'' Wayne.

How Does Coach Jennings' Counseling Strategy Include the Skills and Principals that You Learned in this Program?
Check those that he used:

The Five R's
- ☐ WHY? The Right Purpose
- ☐ Where? The Right Place
- ☐ How? The Right Technique?
- ☐ When? The Right Time
- ☐ What? The Right Approach

The Four Bases
- ☐ Listen—First Base
- ☐ Identify The Problem—Second Base
- ☐ Clarify Alternatives—Third Base
- ☐ Choose and Accept A Solution—Home Base

The Basic Counseling Skills
- ☐ Learn ☐ Accept ☐ Listen ☐ Confirm ☐ Be Optimistic
- ☐ Objectivity ☐ Confidential ☐ Promote Decision-Making ☐ Offer Support

Compare your views with those of the authors on page 57.

LEARNING FROM EXPERIENCE

Counseling isn't something one can learn quickly. Like scuba diving or other demanding sports, the more preparation the better. Experience is necessary to reach high levels of competency. Everytime you counsel you should learn something. Always try to adjust your behavior to accommodate what you have learned so you won't have to relearn it the next time.

AFTER EACH EXPERIENCE, RATE YOURSELF ON HOW TO MAKE IMPROVEMENTS THE NEXT TIME AROUND.

CRITIQUING YOURSELF →

CRITICAL REVIEW

In the months ahead, keep the comparison between baseball and counseling in mind. Make a serious attempt to cover all four bases in each session. To help you remember to do this, please write out (in your own words) what you hope to accomplish at each base. Do this now.

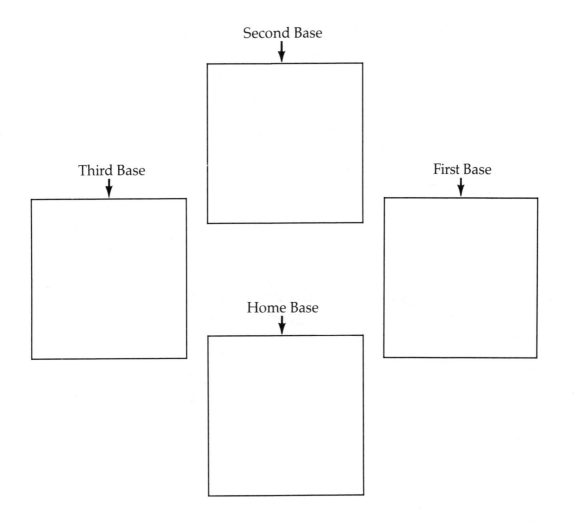

PROFESSIONAL STANDARDS

Almost every aspect of life has certain standards of behavior. Teachers, supervisors, nurses, law officers and others have ethical practices to which they try to conform. Anyone who counsels or advises others should conform to accepted practices of honesty, integrity, and good human relations skills.

DANGERS AHEAD

SIX UNFORGIVABLE MISTAKES

☐ **Acting like a psychologist or clinical counselor when you are not.** The individual might expect therapy, which you are not qualified to deliver.

☐ **Prying into the personal life of the individual you are attempting to help.** It might destroy the counseling relationship.

☐ **Using a counseling relationship to your own advantage.** This violates your primary role as a "helper."

☐ **Failure to keep information obtained from a counseling relationship confidential.** Otherwise you will be labeled as a person who canot be trusted.

☐ **Making decisions for those being counseled.** They won't learn how to make quality decisions. Also if things don't work out, they can blame you.

☐ **Overtalking and underlistening.** You may never learn the real problem.

YOU NEED NOT HAVE FORMAL TRAINING TO BE A GOOD COUNSELOR. DON'T CONFUSE YOUR ROLE HOWEVER WITH PROFESSIONAL CLINICAL COUNSELING. SOME PROBLEMS CAN ONLY BE HANDLED BY EXPERTS.

SUCCESSFUL IDEAS AHEAD

COUNSELING STYLE AND PERSONALITY

With practice, you will develop your own counseling style based on your personality. You need not change your personality to become an effective counselor. You should recognize, however, that different people react differently to the same personality. This means that not all of the people you counsel will react to you in the same way. You may need to give some more time to adjust to you. A few may not adjust well at all. **This should be anticipated.** All counselors, no matter how skilled, have unsuccessful experiences.

The thing to remember is to do your best and learn as you gain experience. Be proud of your counseling style, and be proud of yourself!

To become an excellent counselor, you must **expect** to become one.

COUNSELING STYLE QUIZ

Below are 10 true or false statements. Place a T or F in each square and compare your answers with those at the bottom of the page.

☐ 1. A counselor who is under pressure to complete a session by a certain time is severely handicapped.

☐ 2. Any sexual overtones that develop during a counseling session are distracting and unprofessional.

☐ 3. Counselors are trained to give advice.

☐ 4. Counselors should frequently evaluate themselves to make certain they have not developed irritating habits.

☐ 5. Most people enter into an "intervention" counseling session with some degree of apprehension.

☐ 6. Counselors should quickly terminate a session once the problem has been identified.

☐ 7. In a counseling session, your attitude can speak so loudly the other party cannot hear what you say.

☐ 8. Counseling others should be considered an opportunity and not a job.

☐ 9. The individual being counseled should never be made to feel embarrassed, immature, or guilty.

☐ 10. Only professionals should counsel.

TOTAL CORRECT: ☐

ANSWERS: 1. T (It may not be the right time, and it may be difficult to listen). 2. T (That could distract from the right purpose and may make objectivity difficult. It also could lead to a law suit!) 3. F (They are trained to listen and promote decision-making). 4. T (Failure to establish rapport may prevent an otherwise capable counselor from getting to first base). 5. T (And this makes optimism on your part very important). 6. F (You are only on second base, and you must get to third and home before you score). 7. T (No matter how good your ideas, the client must "hear" to act). 8. T (It should be "mutually rewarding"). 9. T (Listen and accept; don't judge and reject). 10. F (Counseling skills can be used by all of us in our daily lives).

WIN-WIN RELATIONSHIPS

There are times when an open discussion between two people can make both parties winners. In such cases, neither person is a counselor; but if sound counseling techniques are used the discussion will probably be productive.

The long-term success of any human relationship is dependent upon both people coming out ahead. For this to happen, there must be somewhat of a balance between the rewards each individual receives from the other. When one party winds up doing too much "giving", the relationship usually deteriorates. The philosophy of an equal reward system is the basis of The Mutual Reward Theory.

When two people can sit down and openly discuss the rewards they can provide each other, the relationship should measurably improve. Both parties should come out ahead.

MRT OPPORTUNITIES

YOU NEED NOT BE IN THE ROLE OF A COUNSELOR TO MAKE THE MOST OF GOOD COUNSELING TECHNIQUES.

MRT COUNSELING EXERCISE

When applied in counseling situations, the Mutual Reward Theory (MRT) can be used to build new relationships, strengthen older ones, and restore those that are impaired. The key to success is an open discussion of the theory itself followed by an evaluation of the existing reward system.

Read the abbreviated cases below, and place a check mark opposite those that you feel could make use of MRT counseling.

☐   1.   Mark's attitude at work has drastically deteriorated. Where once he was a candidate for promotion, his supervisor would now like to see him resign. The supervisor feels it may be too late to save Mark for the organization.

☐   2.   Marsha and her 17-year old daughter love each other dearly but are constantly fighting over trivial matters. Marsha senses the close relationship they once knew may be gone forever.

☐   3.   Dr. Henry, advisor to the high school student council, is at odds with Drake, the student body president. Drake keeps advocating items he knows will irritate Dr. Henry. As a result, council meetings are a disaster and the quality of student activities on campus are far below previous standards.

☐   4.   Susanne has reached the breaking point. For the past year she has held down a demanding job as well as doing 95% of the work around the apartment. Charles pays 50% of expenses, but that's it. Susanne would like to restore a good relationship but sees little hope.

☐   5.   Maria feels the relationship with her father is all give on her part and no understanding on his. Although she would prefer to stay home with her mother and sisters, now that she is 18 and has a good full-time job she is tempted to leave.

The authors feel MRT counseling is appropriate in all five situations. The MRT goals could be: (1) Mark's attitude toward the job improves and the supervisor's attitude toward Mark improves. (2) Neither party wants to fight: both could come out ahead by pulling back. (3) Both are unhappy and the goals of the council are suffering. A reversal *could* take place. (4) If both parties discuss the situation and agree to more equally divide tasks, the situation should improve. (5) As the relationship with her father improves, Maria could feel closer to the rest of the family; the two younger sisters would benefit.

48

REVIEW

BEFORE YOU CONTINUE, TAKE A MINUTE
TO MAKE SURE YOU HAVE THE BASIC
STEPS DOWN PAT.

RATE YOUR COUNSELING SKILLS

As you progress toward becoming an effective, successful counselor, it is a good idea to rate yourself after each session. This form is designed for this purpose. If you rate yourself as a 5 in any category, you are saying that further improvement is not possible; if you rate yourself a 3 or below, you are saying improvement is necessary.

		High				Low
1.	**Approach:** A non-threatening climate was created. Both parties were relaxed and communicated easily. (Right approach)	5	4	3	2	1
2.	**Talking:** The person being counseled did most of the talking and opened up easily. (First base)	5	4	3	2	1
3.	**Listening:** Because I worked to hear what was said, it was possible to identify the problem easily. (Second base)	5	4	3	2	1
4.	**Voice:** I modulated my voice. It was soft, non-irritating and communicated warmth. (Accepting)	5	4	3	2	1
5.	**Identification of problem:** Both parties agreed the true, underlying problem had been uncovered. (Second base/objectivity)	5	4	3	2	1
6.	**Solving problems:** We listed and discussed several alternatives and came up with an ''elegant solution''. (Third base/home base)	5	4	3	2	1
7.	**Questions:** I did my best to ask the right questions at the right time. (Right time/when)	5	4	3	2	1
8.	**Terminating interview:** The session ended in an upbeat manner. The door was left open for the party to return. (Optimistic)	5	4	3	2	1
9.	**Empathy:** Both parties had feelings of understanding for each other. (Rapport)	5	4	3	2	1
10.	**Sensitivity:** I was sensitive to the needs, feelings, and behavior of the person being counseled. The individual left the session feeling good. (Supportive)	5	4	3	2	1

THE ESSENCE OF COUNSELING

Counseling is communication. It is talking things over. It is searching for a solution. Because counseling deals with feelings it is a sensitive process. Although counseling does not always work, in many situations it offers the best hope for a solution. Even when a solution is not forthcoming, those involved may be able to live with the situation with more grace. There is little to lose.

Yet, despite the hope counseling offers, many hesitate to use the approach. Knowing *why* you avoid the process can help you initiate it more often and improve not only your career but also your life.

On the following page are some common excuses people use for not making the most of counseling.

WHY PEOPLE DELAY

Please place a checkmark in those squares opposite reasons why you might hesitate to use counseling as a technique.

- ☐ Let sleeping dogs lie.
- ☐ Time will solve the problem.
- ☐ I can't keep my emotions out of the process.
- ☐ I'm afraid I'll open up a can of worms.
- ☐ I may say the wrong thing
- ☐ Getting things started bothers me.
- ☐ I have little faith in counseling.
- ☐ I'm uncomfortable in the role of a counselor.
- ☐ Others may laugh at my amateurish approach.
- ☐ I'm not good at communicating.
- ☐ I don't like arguments.
- ☐ The risk is greater than the reward.
- ☐ There is too much involved to do it right.
- ☐ It is just not my thing.
- ☐ I'm afraid I'll get in too deep.

IF, AT ANY TIME, YOU SENSE YOU ARE OVER YOUR HEAD TRYING TO HELP OTHERS SOLVE A PROBLEM, SAY SO AND THEN HELP THEM MAKE A CONNECTION WITH A PROFESSIONAL. SOME INDIVIDUALS MAY HAVE PROBLEMS YOU ARE NOT PREPARED TO DEAL WITH.

MAKE THIS
YOUR PERSONAL
SUCCESS FORMULA

→

SOME FAIL TO BECOME EFFECTIVE
COUNSELORS BECAUSE THEY FORGET THE
FUNDAMENTALS. THE FORMULA ON THE NEXT
PAGE WILL ACT AS A REMINDER TO HELP YOU
SUCCEED AND BECOME INCREASINGLY
PROFESSIONAL IN THE DAYS AHEAD.

COUNSELING SUCCESS FORMULA

Take
Pride in
Doing a
Professional Job

Help Others Feel
Better About Themselves

Show Sensitivity and Support

Cover All Four Bases in Each Counseling
Session

Utilize the Five R's of Why, When, Where, What and How
in Each and Every Counseling Session

Use The Basic Counseling Skills of: Learning, Accepting, Listening,
Confirming, Optimism, Objectivity, Confidence, Promoting Decision-
Making and Offering Support

SUMMARY

IT IS NOW TIME TO MEASURE THE
PROGRESS YOU HAVE MADE.
ON THE FOLLOWING PAGE ARE 20
STATEMENTS WHICH ARE EITHER TRUE
OR FALSE. EACH IS WORTH 5 POINTS.
ANSWERS WILL BE FOUND ON
PAGE 56.

SCORE YOURSELF

DEMONSTRATE YOUR PROGRESS

For each statement below, put a check under true or false.

True False

_____ _____ 1. Counseling is primarily problem solving.

_____ _____ 2. Selecting the *right* person is one of the 5 R's of counseling.

_____ _____ 3. Becoming a good counselor should measurably improve your career progress.

_____ _____ 4. Few people have the right stuff to become good counselors.

_____ _____ 5. The less talking you do as a counselor the more effective you will be.

_____ _____ 6. Intervention counseling is very difficult.

_____ _____ 7. Only highly trained professionals should counsel.

_____ _____ 8. A good counselor is one who helps others find elegant solutions to their problems.

_____ _____ 9. The job of the counselor is to weigh alternatives and let the person being counseled make the decision.

_____ _____ 10. MRT works best when the counselor tries to maintain a long-term, healthy relationship with the other party.

_____ _____ 11. Sometimes individuals need to blame others before they admit they are responsible.

_____ _____ 12. Acting like a psychologist or clinical counselor is not one of the unforgivable mistakes.

_____ _____ 13. To become a good counselor one must go through a personality change.

_____ _____ 14. Quiet people, even those with great confidence, seldom become successful counselors.

_____ _____ 15. The best place to identify a person's problem is on home base.

_____ _____ 16. No matter how a session turns out, a skillful counselor always makes the other party feel better.

_____ _____ 17. Without a positive attitude, becoming a good counselor is impossible.

_____ _____ 18. Most counselors fail because of insensitive behavior.

_____ _____ 19. The way to become a professional counselor is to analyze mistakes after each session and then make behavioral changes so the mistakes are not repeated.

_____ _____ 20. To make maximum use of this program you should study and review it often.

☐ TOTAL   Turn page for answers.

1. T — In order to work, you must get around all four bases.

2. F — The person is **a given**. The five R's are why and how you go about counseling.

3. T — Counseling skills are basic to good management.

4. F — It simply takes a desire to help people along with good "common sense".

5. T — The most important counseling skill is **listening**; the least important is **giving advice**.

6. T — It is easier (but less effective) to sit back and wait for a solution.

7. F — Most intelligent adults possess the skills to help people solve problems.

8. T — Too often counselors are advice-givers rather than solution-seekers.

9. T — The person should make his or her own decision.

10. T — A relationship where both continue to benefit.

11. T — A good counselor can help an individual get beyond this stage.

12. F — You must be realistic about what you are qualified to do.

13. F — Your best personality is the one you were born with.

14. F — Confidence is much more important for a counselor than verbal skills.

15. F — It is second base.

16. T — A major counseling task is to promote self-esteem.

17. T — Your attitude is always communicated.

18. T — Such as talking too much.

19. T — Constant review is essential.

20. T — But you also must begin to actually counsel.

AUTHOR'S SUGGESTED ANSWERS TO CASES

Who will make the best counselor? Although both Byron and Ginger could become outstanding counselors, the authors feel Ginger may have a better chance because she will not permit her ambitions to get in the way. Byron appears to be so ambitious and ego-centered that he may have trouble relaxing to the point where he could do a sensitive job of counseling. He might lose patience and attempt to impose his solutions on others.

Which approach is best? All three approaches could conceivably work (depending upon Justine's skills as a counselor) but the authors prefer approach #3 because it is more problem-centered than the others. Sally's on-the-job future depends upon her ability to balance her home and career. This is a difficult problem and alternatives need to be explored. Approach #3 leads quickly to ''getting around the bases''.

Will Gray get to second base with his son? Gray is in a tight spot. His strategy and techniques to get to second base appear excellent, but success may depend more upon his past relationship than anything else. The most difficult person to counsel is often the person closest to you. Talking over what he feels to be the best solution with his ex-wife is vital to avoid Tony playing one parent against the other.

A challenge for the counselor. The authors rate Reverend Stacy as an excellent counselor. He appears to have the skill of guiding others toward an elegant solution and then back away from making it himself. In this instance, he provides additional time to discuss alternatives. Chances are good the Jones will come up with the best solution and live with it gracefully.

Counseling strategy. Coach Jennings seems to be coming up with too little too late. It is difficult to understand why he has not counseled Wayne on the problem as it developed. Perhaps the coach lacks confidence in his counseling skills. Wayne *needs* guidance and would probably accept it if done with sensitivity. Problems seldom solve themselves. Coach Jennings ''game plan'' to bench Wayne if he doesn't do a turnaround within a week could cause the coach to be over-threatening. More flexibility is recommended.

APPLICATION OF YOUR NEW
COUNSELING SKILLS

The sooner you apply what you have learned the better. It is recommended that you set up two or three counseling situations as soon as it is practical. Before you enter into each session, review this FIFTY MINUTE PROGRAM. After you have finished, complete the critique on page 49. Practice may not make you perfect, but it will help.

APPLICATION OF COUNSELING SKILLS

Name of **person with whom** you will be working:

_____

5 R's:

      Purpose of session: _____

      Time scheduled: _____

      Place:_____

      Approach you intend to use: _____

      Techniques, general strategy: _____

      _____

      _____

      _____

      _____

      _____

      _____

      _____

(This form may be copied)

APPLICATION OF COUNSELING SKILLS

Name of person with whom you will be working:

_____

5 R's:

       Purpose of session: _____

       Time scheduled: _____

       Place:_____

       Approach you intend to use: _____

       Techniques, general strategy: _____

       _____

       _____

       _____

       _____

       _____

       _____

       _____

(This form may be copied)

NOTES

ABOUT THE FIFTY-MINUTE SERIES

"Fifty-Minute books are the best new publishing idea in years. They are clear, practical, concise and affordable — perfect for today's world."

Leo Hauser
(Past President, ASTD)

What Is A Fifty-Minute Book?

—Fifty-Minute books are brief, soft-cover, "self-study" modules which cover a single concept. They are reasonably priced, and ideal for formal training programs, excellent for self-study and perfect for remote location training.

Why Are Fifty-Minute Books Unique?

—Because of their format and level. Designed to be "read with a pencil," the basics of a subject can be quickly grasped and applied through a series of hands-on activities, exercises and cases.

How Many Fifty-Minute Books Are There?

—Those listed on the facing page at this time, however, additional titles are in development. For more information write to **Crisp Publications, Inc., 95 First Street, Los Altos, CA 94022.**

Crisp books are distributed in Canada by Reid Publishing, Ltd., P.O. Box 7267, Oakville, Ontario, Canada L6J 6L6.

In Australia by Career Builders, P.O. Box 1051 Springwood, Brisbane, Queensland, Australia 4127.

And in New Zealand by Career Builders, P.O. Box 571, Manurewa, New Zealand.

THE FIFTY-MINUTE SERIES

Quantity	Title	Code #	Price	Amount
	MANAGEMENT TRAINING			
	Self-Managing Teams	000-0	$7.95	
	Delegating For Results	008-6	$7.95	
	Successful Negotiation—Revised	09-2	$7.95	
	Increasing Employee Productivity	010-8	$7.95	
	Personal Performance Contracts—Revised	12-2	$7.95	
	Team Building—Revised	16-5	$7.95	
	Effective Meeting Skills	33-5	$7.95	
	An Honest Day's Work: Motivating Employees To Excel	39-4	$7.95	
	Managing Disagreement Constructively	41-6	$7.95	
	Training Managers To Train	43-2	$7.95	
	The Fifty-Minute Supervisor—Revised	58-0	$7.95	
	Leadership Skills For Women	62-9	$7.95	
	Systematic Problem Solving & Decision Making	63-7	$7.95	
	Coaching & Counseling	68-8	$7.95	
	Ethics In Business	69-6	$7.95	
	Understanding Organizational Change	71-8	$7.95	
	Project Management	75-0	$7.95	
	Risk Taking	76-9	$7.95	
	Managing Organizational Change	80-7	$7.95	
	Working Together In A Multi-Cultural Organization	85-8	$7.95	
	Selecting a Consultant	87-4	$7.95	
	PERSONNEL MANAGEMENT			
	Your First Thirty Days: A Professional Image in a New Job	003-5	$7.95	
	Office Management	005-1	$7.95	
	Attacking Absentism	042-6	$7.95	
	Men and Women: Partners at Work	009-4	$7.95	
	Effective Performance Appraisals—Revised	11-4	$7.95	
	Quality Interviewing—Revised	13-0	$7.95	
	Personal Counseling	14-9	$7.95	
	New Employee Orientation	46-7	$7.95	
	Professional Excellence For Secretaries	52-1	$7.95	
	Guide To Affirmative Action	54-8	$7.95	
	Writing A Human Resources Manual	70-X	$7.95	
	Winning at Human Relations	86-6	$7.95	
	WELLNESS			
	Mental Fitness	15-7	$7.95	
	Wellness in the Workplace	020-5	$7.95	
	Personal Wellness	021-3	$7.95	
	Preventing Job Burnout	23-8	$7.95	

THE FIFTY-MINUTE SERIES (Continued)

Quantity	Title	Code #	Price	Amount
	WELLNESS (CONTINUED)			
	Job Performance and Chemical Dependency	27-0	$7.95	
	Overcoming Anxiety	029-9	$7.95	
	Productivity at the Workstation	041-8	$7.95	
	COMMUNICATIONS			
	Technical Writing	004-3	$7.95	
	Giving and Receiving Criticism	023-X	$7.95	
	Effective Presentation Skills	24-6	$7.95	
	Better Business Writing—Revised	25-4	$7.95	
	The Business Of Listening	34-3	$7.95	
	Writing Fitness	35-1	$7.95	
	The Art Of Communicating	45-9	$7.95	
	Technical Presentation Skills	55-6	$7.95	
	Making Humor Work	61-0	$7.95	
	Visual Aids In Business	77-7	$7.95	
	Speed-Reading In Business	78-5	$7.95	
	Publicity Power	82-3	$7.95	
	SELF-MANAGEMENT			
	Attitude: Your Most Priceless Possession-Revised	011-6	$7.95	
	Personal Time Management	22-X	$7.95	
	Successful Self-Management	26-2	$7.95	
	Business Etiquette	032-9	$7.95	
	Balancing Home And Career—Revised	035-3	$7.95	
	Developing Positive Assertiveness	38-6	$7.95	
	Time Management And The Telephone	53-X	$7.95	
	Memory Skills In Business	56-4	$7.95	
	Developing Self-Esteem	66-1	$7.95	
	Creativity In Business	67-X	$7.95	
	Managing Personal Change	74-2	$7.95	
	Stop Procrastinating: Get To Work!	88-2	$7.95	
	CUSTOMER SERVICE/SALES TRAINING			
	Sales Training Basics—Revised	02-5	$7.95	
	Restaurant Server's Guide—Revised	08-4	$7.95	
	Telephone Courtesy And Customer Service	18-1	$7.95	
	Effective Sales Management	031-0	$7.95	
	Professional Selling	42-4	$7.95	
	Customer Satisfaction	57-2	$7.95	
	Telemarketing Basics	60-2	$7.95	
	Calming Upset Customers	65-3	$7.95	
	Quality At Work	72-6	$7.95	
	Managing Quality Customer Service	83-1	$7.95	
	Quality Customer Service—Revised	95-5	$7.95	
	SMALL BUSINESS AND FINANCIAL PLANNING			
	Becoming A Consultant	006-X	$7.95	
	Basic Business Financial Analysis	022-1	$7.95	
	Effective Collection Techniques	034-5	$7.95	
	Marketing Your Consulting Or Professional Services	40-8	$7.95	

THE FIFTY-MINUTE SERIES (Continued)

Quantity	Title	Code #	Price	Amount
	SMALL BUSINESS AND FINANCIAL PLANNING (CONTINUED)			
	Starting Your New Business	44-0	$7.95	
	Personal Financial Fitness—Revised	89-0	$7.95	
	BASIC LEARNING SKILLS			
	Returning To Learning: Getting A G.E.D.	002-7	$7.95	
	Study Skills Strategies—Revised	05-X	$7.95	
	Basic Business Math	024-8	$7.95	
	Becoming An Effective Tutor	028-0	$7.95	
	CAREER PLANNING			
	Career Discovery	07-6	$7.95	
	Networking Your Way to Success	030-2	$7.95	
	Preparing for Your Interview	033-7	$7.95	
	Plan B: Protecting Your Career	48-3	$7.95	
	I Got the Job!	59-9	$7.95	
	RETIREMENT			
	Personal Financial Fitness—Revised	89-0	$7.95	
	Financial Planning	90-4	$7.95	
	## OTHER CRISP INC. BOOKS			
	Stepping Up To Supervisor	11-8	$13.95	
	The Unfinished Business Of Living: Helping Aging Parents	19-X	$12.95	
	Managing Performance	23-7	$19.95	
	Be True To Your Future: A Guide To Life Planning	47-5	$13.95	
	Up Your Productivity	49-1	$10.95	
	Comfort Zones: Planning Your Future 2/e	73-4	$13.95	
	Copyediting 2/e	94-7	$18.95	
	Practical Time Management	275-4	$13.95	

VIDEO TITLE*

Quantity		Code #	Preview	Purchase	Amount
	Video Title*				
	Attitude: Your Most Priceless Possession	012-4	$25.00	$395.00	
	Quality Customer Service	013-2	$25.00	$395.00	
	Team Building	014-2	$25.00	$395.00	
	Job Performance & Chemical Dependency	015-9	$25.00	$395.00	
	Better Business Writing	016-7	$25.00	$395.00	
	Creativity in Business	036-1	$25.00	$395.00	
	Honest Day's Work	037-X	$25.00	$395.00	
	Calming Upset Customers	040-X	$25.00	$395.00	
	Balancing Home and Career	048-5	$25.00	$395.00	
	Mental Fitness	049-3	$25.00	$395.00	

(*Note: All tapes are VHS format. Video package includes five books and a Leader's Guide.)

	Amount
Total Books	
Less Discount (5 or more different books 20% sampler)	
Total Videos	
Less Discount (purchase of 3 or more videos earn 20%)	
Shipping ($3.50 per video, $.50 per book)	
California Tax (California residents add 7%)	
TOTAL	

☐ Send volume discount information.   ☐ Please send me a catalog.

☐ Please charge the following credit card   ☐ Mastercard   ☐ VISA   ☐ AMEX

Account No. _____ Name (as appears on card) _____

Ship to: _____   Bill to: _____

_____   _____

_____   _____

_____   _____

Phone number: _____   P.O. # _____

All orders except those with a P.O.# must be prepaid.
For more information Call (415) 949-4888 or FAX (415) 949-1610.

NOTES

NOTES